Praise for *Happiness Matters*

Beenie is onto the secret recipe of happiness. Someone who stumbles on this wisdom and applies it might accidentally create a very fulfilling life! Her vulnerability opens the door for all of us to stop making excuses for why we're not happy, to own our past, to extend forgiveness, and to live wholeheartedly into the future.

Donna Carlson
360 Life Strategy Coach

This book is about taking the journey from not loving yourself to learning to love and accept yourself for who you are. It reminds us that we are not responsible for others' actions, and we should never blame ourselves for their behavior. We can control our emotions and our happiness, and we are responsible for the decision to be happy.

Robin Depies
Financial Advisor

Happiness Matters is a short yet impactful read. This book allowed me to reflect on the one thing that I've lacked in years past, and that is self-love. I encourage readers to do a self-evaluation and self-reflection on their self-love. It may just be the determining factor and the breakthrough to true Happiness.

Emerald Taylor
Business Consultant for the Purpose Driven Woman

Beenie's guidance is simplistic, practical, and IMPACTFUL! She has a magical way of describing and connecting everyday examples (highways, rivers, etc.) to higher level transformation. She demystifies the concepts and breaks them down into realistic, definable, and digestible pieces. Beenie's story is real, and it brought tears to my heart; however, her confidence is CONTAGIOUS, and you can't help but feel EMPOWERED, POWERFUL, and like "I've GOT this!" Beenie, thank you for sharing.

Liz Killen-Scott
Transformation Consultant
BeingHR Consulting

Beenie Mann takes us on a quest through our ego-system and empowers us to cultivate our own sustainable eco-system of happiness. We take an inspiring walk with her on her own courageous superhero's journey. Through the example of her vulnerably and grace, we begin to believe we can fly! This is one of the few books that simplifies how we truly craft our own reality and helps us to create, allow, and embrace happiness in our lives.

Tamara Moore
Founding CEO
Relevel, LLC

Happiness Matters *is both a thoughtful delivery of a powerful message (use your superpower of Happiness to live a fruitful life) and an insightful account of 7 factors that serve as a guide to do so. Beenie Mann is an amazing lady who has always put others first and continues to do so in delivering this personal and purposeful book. I am proud to call her friend.*

Colonel Robert F. McLaughlin
U.S Army, Retired
Chief Operating Officer
Mt. Carmel Veterans Service Center

Happiness Matters

Unleash Your Superpower in 7 Easy Steps

Beenie Mann

Good Spirit Publishing

Happiness Matters: Unleash Your Superpower in 7 Easy Steps

Copyright © 2018 by Sabine (Beenie) Mann

Cover Design – Akash Ghosh
Editor – Nina Durfee
Author Photo – Jay Billups Photography

All rights reserved. No part of this book may be reproduced or transmitted in any form or by any means without written permission from the author. This includes reprints, excerpts, photocopying, recording, or any further means of reproducing text. Contact Sabine (Beenie) Mann through her website, www.BeenieMann.com

The material in this book is intended for education. It is not meant to take the place of diagnosis and treatment by a qualified medical practitioner or therapist. No guarantee of the effects of using the recommendations can be given, nor liability taken.

ISBN 978-1-7324801-1-7

Printed in USA

To Jeff, Tim, and Patrick.
I love you *immer zweimal mehr*.

Acknowledgments

Like so many great productions, this book wouldn't be here without some amazing people in my life. Some stopped in for a little while, others stayed and are holding on. Thank you all.

A huge thank you to my incredible husband who is always supporting and encouraging me. Thank you, Schatzi, for always letting me fly and having my back. You are the star of my noodle soup and I love you *grosse proportions*.

My boys, Timothy and Patrick—you make a momma proud, and you rock my world. Thank you for teaching me patience, forgiving me, and being such incredible cheerleaders. I love you to infinity and beyond!

Leilani, so happy to have you as my "daughter-in-love." You are a powerful inspiration and one of the strongest women I know. I love you!

Barbara Harrington, my friend, you truly opened up the Universe to me. Thank you for all your teachings, support, friendship, and occasional kick in the rear.

A huge thank you to my friend Rachel Stovall for your encouragement, your belief in me, and your friendship.

My editor, Nina Durfee—you are simply the best. Thank you for your guidance and patience.

My book cover designer, Akash Ghosh – your incredible talent in bringing life to my vision is awe-inspiring.

Table of Contents

Introduction vi

What is Happiness 1

Step 1: Gratitude 9

Step 2: Forgiveness 21

Step 3: Love Yourself 35

Step 4: Nurture Your Subconscious 49

Step 5: Mindset 63

Step 6: Go with the Flow 77

Step 7: Have Fun 91

7 Steps to Happiness 103

About the Author 105

Introduction

Happiness—the most underused superpower we each possess. Humans want to be happy, safe, and loved. Why do some seem to be happy all the time, while others are not? Why do some seem to have unlocked their superpower while others struggle to release theirs?

Happiness, in my opinion and experience, is the key to success, better relationships, better health, and an overall better outlook on life. It truly is a superpower and the key to fulfillment.

In this book I share the keys that aided me to find and unleash my happiness in spite of all I endured growing up and beyond. Each chapter will reveal different incidents of my life and how I was able to overcome the obstacles thrown at me.

Like others, I have dealt with dark times, pain, abuse, and more. I've discovered it is possible to overcome, to shine, and yes, to be truly happy. I hope that my story will inspire you to overcome obstacles and live a life of happiness.

Every superhero has a superpower. You are the superhero in your story, and happiness is your yet untapped superpower!

May these 7 easy steps guide you to unleash your superpower and live happily ever after.

Choose happy. Be happy. Be kind. Share your smile and make the world a better place.

What is Happiness?

"Happiness cannot be traveled to, owned, earned, worn, or consumed. Happiness is the spiritual experience of living every minute with love, grace, and gratitude."
Denis Waitley

happiness
noun – hap·pi·ness / ˈhapēnəs/
- a state of well-being and contentment
- a pleasurable or satisfying experience

Before I share the 7 steps, let's define happiness.

Is happiness the same as contentment? If not, what's the difference? How do we know if we are content or happy?

Great question, and opinions vary widely. Consider this:

For a very long time I thought I was happy, because I was content with my life and myself. The two terms seemed interchangeable. Being content meant being happy. And because I thought I was happy, I was content. But was I? Are you?

For myself, being content means making the best of a situation so it will work for me. Being content means basic needs are met, with added elements to make it fun. Contentment feels peaceful. It feels calm. It feels safe.

Happiness, on the other hand, is an emotion that makes my whole body light up and puts a giant smile on my face. Happiness feels like the biggest, brightest, and best vibration, the vibration I want to send out to the universe.

Why am I bringing vibration into the conversation? Simple. Everything is energy, and everything vibrates.

<u>Law of Vibration.</u> Everything in the universe moves, vibrates, and travels in circular patterns. The same principles of vibration in the physical world apply to our thoughts, feelings, desires, and wills in the etheric world. Each sound, thing, and even thought has its own vibrational frequency, unique unto itself.

Are you familiar with the saying, "Misery loves company"? The feeling of misery is energy vibrating at a very low level. Vibrations resonate with whatever possesses identical frequency. This means our thoughts are inseparably connected to the rest of the universe. "Like attracts like."

Law of Attraction. The Law of Attraction demonstrates why we experience the things, events, and people that come into our lives. Our thoughts, feelings, words, and actions consist of energy which, in turn, attracts like energy. Negative energies attract negative energies, and positive energies attract positive energies.

The Law of Attraction applies to our happy vibration! When we vibrate at a higher level, we attract better things, people, and circumstances. How wonderful! More good stuff in our life adds to our happiness.

Did you notice how I said "adds" to our happiness? The truth is, nothing and nobody can make you happy or unhappy. You alone have the power to be happy. Happiness is a choice! It is not a thing, a circumstance, or a person or outside influence. Only you can make that choice. Let that sink in.

You alone have the power over your happiness.

Happiness is an inside job.

WOW! Once this sunk in for me, my whole world changed. I'm not saying everything is hunky dory all the time. I'm saying I have a new appreciation of what is happening to and around me. Because I come from a place of deep-rooted happiness, I am able to deal with and manage better what life has in store for me. Since I choose happiness, I have more good experiences, good people, and good things coming my way.

Once you have discovered and chosen your happiness, you will notice more of the positive and brighter things in every situation. Not only will you bounce back more easily when you have been knocked down, you will get up faster.

When you choose happiness, you notice more positive and pleasant things in your life. You feel uplifted by happiness. Your outlook on life changes. Trust me when I tell you, life is much more fun viewed through the lens of happiness versus the lens of despair.

Have you ever searched the Internet for the term "happiness" or "how to be happy"? The results are overwhelming—there is a ton of information, tips, tricks, and whatnot.

I had no good role models growing up, so when I was about to be a mom for the first time, I had to look elsewhere for information. I resorted to books, friends, and TV programs. Yup, no internet for my first pregnancy. (Boy, did I just age myself!)

My point is, I did research—a lot of research—on how to be a good parent and what to expect. Most of the information was fantastic. However, I had to sift through and find what would work for me and my personality.

The same is true for you and your pursuit of your happiness. Already you have done some digging. You bought this book. You've probably asked some questions and dabbled in this and that. Keep at it. Even though I have found my happiness, I continue to research how I can enhance it even more.

Life is a journey. Enjoy the ride. Find the joy, beauty, or lesson in everything. Let happiness be the vehicle you drive on your journey of life. It is your journey. Take command of the driver's seat. Choose your direction. I have taken some wrong turns, and still do on occasion. But being in charge of my journey empowers me to change direction at will. You have this power, too.

Did this help you determine if you are happy or content? Whatever your state of being, I hope the seven easy steps in this book will help you to unleash and grow your incredible superpower. Take these steps in any order. We are all on different paths in our individual journeys. But the paths build on top of each other, and all are equally important.

Let the journey begin!

"To be happy or not to be. The choice is yours."

Beenie Mann

Notes and Thoughts

What does happiness mean to you?

Step 1: **Gratitude**

"Develop an attitude of gratitude, and give thanks for everything that happens to you, knowing that every step forward is a step toward achieving something bigger and better than your current situation."
Brian Tracy

gratitude
noun - grat·i·tude / ˈgradə‚t(y)o͞od/
- a strong feeling of appreciation to someone or something for what the person has done to help you

Attitude of gratitude. We have heard the phrase many times, but what does it actually mean? You may have been raised to say "please'" and "thank you" when appropriate. When you say those words, is it genuine, or is it an automatic, trained response?

Do we say "please" and "thank you" because it is the norm and is expected? Is it because we were taught those words as a set of good manners? Or are we consciously aware when we say those words?

There's nothing wrong with good programming. We live in a society with rules and norms to live by. Rules and norms help us feel safe and be safe. Norms and rules are generally good.

What do you feel when you say "thank you"? Do you feel anything? You might be wondering, "What am I supposed to feel?" It took me a long time to grasp. Coaches and motivational speakers talk about gratitude and how we are supposed to have this positive attitude around it. Always be grateful, they say. There is something to be grateful for in every situation, they say. There is at least one good aspect you can focus on and build on, they say.

But what do they know about me and my circumstances? They don't know what it's like. They have never been through what I have been through or am going through right now. They don't have my worries. They don't have a clue about me and my experience. They don't know what I have lived through. It's easy for them to say I can find something positive in my situation.

Can you relate?

It is impossible to find something positive, something to be grateful for in my situation. I am a victim here. I am in this situation at no fault of my own. I am just trying to keep my *head above water, and I do not see anything positive that could be used as a life raft. I am drowning!*

Sound familiar?

A big issue for me was feeling overwhelmed and having a victim mentality. I threw the best pity parties for myself, coming up with every excuse for my situation and why I couldn't escape. It was gloom and doom. Occasionally a ray of sunshine would peek through my storm, but it was always short-lived. I always waited for the other shoe to drop. And of course, it dropped, sending me deeper into my victimhood.

I grew up being afraid. I was afraid of my mother. I was afraid of her unpredictability and what it would mean for me. My parents divorced when I was six. My father left and felt no obligation to support his only child. That left my mother as a single parent, barely able to make ends meet.

From the beginning, my mother never wanted me. For her, I was the means to an end. At seventeen she decided to get pregnant so my father would marry her and take her out of her parents' house. It worked. She became pregnant, he married her, and they moved in together.

I don't remember much before the big fight that ended their marriage, but boy, do I remember that day! The screaming, yelling, and furniture smashing drove me to hide under a desk, scared out of my mind. I was a little six-year-old girl trying desperately not to get caught in the crossfire of the people who were supposed to love and protect me.

Somehow, I survived. After my father left and my mother was stuck with me, she made it clear I was neither wanted nor loved. The constant bombardment of "you are just like your father," "you are no good," "I never wanted you anyway," "you are ugly," "you are fat"—those epithets were my constant companions.

And there were beatings. Sometimes it felt as if my mother was looking for a reason to beat the daylight out of me in order to relieve her built-up frustrations. When I was a teenager, she pounded on me in the bathroom because I didn't clean the sink exactly as she wanted it. She laid into me with the side of her hand. I held my arms up to protect my face and head as much as I could. For weeks I wore a deep purple belt of bruises around my back and sides. The physical bruises were deep. The emotional scars were deeper and lasted for decades.

Growing up was not fun. It was rough and it was dark. I was in constant fear and longed to be loved. I especially wanted to be loved by the one person who is supposed to love me unconditionally. If my own mother couldn't love me, who could?

I managed to get away from her when I was seventeen. No, I did not get pregnant. History did not repeat itself. After failing tenth grade, I lost an apprenticeship, and my mother gave me an ultimatum: either find work, or go to boarding school. I chose boarding school! Since she was a single parent and I had already reached out to child social services, it was no issue for me to find a school. The City of Stuttgart picked up the tab.

Boarding school was my saving grace! I was fortunate to be there for five years. The longest you can go to school in Germany is thirteen years, but since I had flunked tenth grade, I was required to repeat it. I liked it so much at the school that I flunked my last year and had to repeat that as well. No, I didn't flunk on purpose. It was more like the Universe knew I was angry and not ready to move out into the world. At the time I wasn't too thrilled, but now I know it was in my best interest to stay an extra year.

Those five years in boarding school were my best five years growing up. For the first time in my life, I wasn't afraid. For the first time in those five years, people liked and cared for me. For the first time, I learned that I mattered.

I was slow to make friends. I didn't understand the concept of friendship, treating each other with respect and care. It took a very long time, beyond boarding school, for me to trust people. It took a very long time for me to "let people in."

My classmates and teachers helped me break down my wall of protection. They helped me find glimmers of hope shining through more and more. They taught me that I mattered. They taught me I was worthy. They taught me I was lovable. They taught me to become me.

What does all this have to do with gratitude? Well, because of those five years at boarding school, I allowed myself to heal. It didn't happen overnight. It didn't happen during those years at the school. It took a long while. Even to this day, there are times the very thin skin that now covers my scars breaks open a tiny bit. And that is okay.

It took some therapy with more loving and caring people to chisel away that wall. The more they were able to break it down, the more it built me up. I finally learned to trust a little. Love a little. Smile more. Feel safe.

When I met my husband, I no longer hated myself. By then I had attained the level of simply not liking myself. He came in and kicked down what was left of my wall. He showed me (and still does) unconditional love. To this day he tells me he loves me, how beautiful I am, and how proud of me he is.

Something inside of me started to sprout. It was a strange feeling. What was this new sensation? It wasn't love, although that was there too. The new sensation was contentment. I started to feel very safe and very loved. I started to believe that more goodness was coming.

The birth of our boys took me to a whole new level of good feeling and emotion. Holding our oldest for the first time was the most overwhelming, scary, and exciting moment of my life. I loved my husband at a level I never knew possible. Holding my son, I thought I would explode. I was so full of love!

This feeling of contentment grew. It kept on blossoming but it never really came to full bloom, at least not for a few more years. During those years, in addition to seeing a counselor, I did a lot of personal development. During that time, I learned the meaning of gratitude.

Gratitude was a completely new concept for me. How can I be grateful if I am still licking my wounds?

One day, I watched *Oprah*, and that show was a game-changer for me. The whole show was about gratitude. Oprah talked about a gratitude journal. What the heck was that? I was intrigued and hung on her every word.

She suggested writing down ten things I was grateful for each night before bed—not from the day prior, not what tomorrow might bring, only that current day. Challenge accepted!

Turns out, it was a lot easier said than done, especially since those very dark days still haunted me. The first four, five, or even six things were easy to list. I could always find a handful of things and situations to be grateful for. But ramping up the list to ten things was difficult.

I was grateful for being alive, for my kids, my husband, the blue skies that day, a compliment I received. Those were easy! For the last few, I had to dig, and I had to dig deep. Oh, I saw a pretty butterfly today, I am grateful for him. The neighbor not playing their music too loud, I can be grateful for that too. Ants not infesting my kitchen like they did for the people next door. You get the point.

This exercise is powerful to help you find gratitude even in the simplest of things. Diligently, each night I wrote down the ten things I was grateful for that day. No copying the ones from the day prior; you need to dig deep. In the beginning, it took me awhile to complete my list of ten each day. Not only did I write them down, but I also read them out loud. The next morning, I read them out loud again to help me start my day on a positive note.

Shortly after I started this exercise, it became easier and easier to find my ten. Hmmm ... what is going on? Soon I upped my number to twenty. You see, once ten stopped being a challenge, I lost the good feeling that came from digging deep to find ten. So, I went to twenty, then to thirty, and eventually I formed new neural pathways.

Since I knew I had to complete my list in the evening, I started to pay more attention during the day. Slowly but surely my focus shifted. Before I started the exercise, I was focused on the negative occurrences around me. Now I am more and more focused on the positive.

What does my story teach about gratitude? Today I am happy to tell you I am grateful for every bit of the crap I had to go through as a kid and young adult. For if it wasn't for all that crap, I would not be the person I am today.

I am grateful for the lessons my mother taught me. She was an incredible, sad excuse of a parent; she taught me how not to parent. She taught me on so many levels what not to do. For those lessons, I am grateful.

She has taught me empathy and compassion—not by her example, but because of what I had to endure. It helped me to connect with others who suffered. By focusing on and comforting others, I was able to forget about my own misery for a little while.

I am grateful for my absolutely amazing husband and boys, for they have taught me that I am worth it. I am loved. I matter!

Today I am grateful for everything and everyone I encounter, for each is teaching me something. Today the blossom of gratitude is in full bloom and growing.

Don't get me wrong. My mind still drifts off into negative thought patterns. After all, I am human. But I don't stay there, and you don't have to either.

Once you pay attention to where your thoughts drift and you catch yourself feeling sorry for yourself, stop. Take a deep breath and find something to be grateful for. Make a mental note, as you will need it in the evening when you complete your list of ten.

Count your blessings. Be grateful.

What are you grateful for today, right now in this moment? How does it make you feel? Does it make you smile and your heart sing? Does it make your heart beat a little faster? Does it lift you up? That's gratitude.

"Gratitude unlocks the fullness of life. It turns what we have into enough, and more. It turns denial into acceptance, chaos to order, confusion to clarity. It can turn a meal into a feast, a house into a home, a stranger into a friend."
Melody Beattie

Notes and Thoughts

What are you grateful for?

Step 2: **Forgiveness**

"The weak can never forgive. Forgiveness is the attribute of the strong."

Mahatma Gandhi

forgiveness
noun - for·give·ness / fər'givnəs/
- the act of forgiving

Forgiveness doesn't excuse behavior. Forgiveness prevents behavior from destroying your heart.

Let these two thoughts sink in for a minute.

Forgiveness is a strange entity. As with anything, forgiveness has many levels. In this chapter, I will dive into deep-rooted, painful forgiveness. It is easy to forgive somebody who bumped into your body or your car. This is not the kind of forgiveness that evokes happiness.

Happiness depends on the capacity to forgive those who have inflicted deep emotional and physical scars upon you. I am talking about the wounds that took you deep into the abyss and left you wounded and crippled, physically and emotionally.

Humans experience pain on different levels, because we are each unique. We have various physical pain thresholds. What one experiences as a level two, another might experience as a level seven. This does not mean one is stronger or weaker than the other. It simply means we all experience pain differently.

The same is true with emotional pain. One person can endure more than another before reaching a breaking point. I believe we all have our breaking point, and it's different for each person. No matter when it comes, the breaking point is painful, and we tend to carry that pain with us. It's easy to blame the person who inflicted the pain and retreat into victimhood.

I get it. For the longest time I blamed my mother for all the misery in my life. I felt sorry for myself. I was a victim. I carried inside of me so much hate and anger toward her for so long. I gave her power over my emotions, my every waking moment, and my life.

I grew up being afraid of her, because I never knew what to expect. I mentioned that she never wanted me in the first place. At one point, she denied my existence completely. Once I knew this, not only did all the old wounds rip wide open again, but this time I felt as if my heart and soul were ripped out and salt poured into the open wounds.

One day I will never forget. I was in my thirties, a wife and a mother. My relationship with my mother was frosty, but I still tried desperately to win her love. I was willing to give her another chance.

We were stationed in Germany, roughly a three-hour car ride away from my home town. We had just moved back to Germany from the States, and I was excited to see old friends and family. One weekend my husband and I decided to grab the kids and jump in the car to visit family.

We arrived at my aunt and uncle's house. It was wonderful to see them. We caught up on our lives and had a great time, until my aunt shared with me that my mother had recently come to visit them with her new love interest. My mother had asked my aunt not to mention to her lover that she had a daughter. Say WHAT???

My jaw dropped; my heart felt like it was being ripped out; and I broke down. My aunt tried to comfort me by "helping" me understand why my mother made this request. *Are you freaking kidding me? How can you justify her totally denying my existence?* It might have been different if I were still a little kid and she didn't want to scare him off by letting the cat out of the bag right away. That I could have dealt with. But at this point I was married with a family of my own, not even living in the same city! At her age did she really think the guy didn't expect her to have a family?

I lost it. I broke down, shaking, sobbing, and hurt far more than I had ever hurt in the past. Honestly, I believe the hurt was so much deeper because my family teamed up to take her side. Thank goodness my husband and kids were with me to wrap me in their arms. They showered unconditional love on me. If it weren't for them, I would have felt completely alone and betrayed.

I took the hurt, the betrayal, and the anger with me that day. I carried it inside for years to come. I used it as an excuse to be a victim and to be miserable. I used it as an excuse to ease my pain with food. I used it as an excuse to lash out to the people closest to me. I used it as an excuse to wallow in self-pity. After all, I was the victim here!

In spite of it all, I put on the happy face to the outside world. I helped others any way I could. My husband was the only person who knew the darkness inside of me. He was there to hold me, wipe the tears, love me, and comfort me. He was my lighthouse.

One day, I came across something about forgiveness, and the seed was planted. I was hurting, and letting my mother have the power of my every waking moment needed to come to an end. I needed the hurt to stop before it destroyed me and everything I had with my husband and kids.

The question was HOW? How do I make it stop and take my power back? How can I forgive that woman who has used, abused, and hurt me over and over? Was it even possible?

I had to find out and at least give it a try.

The best way to get answers is to research. By that time we had a computer and internet service. It yielded results faster than traipsing to the library.

Even though the magnitude of online information back then wasn't what it is today, there was plenty to get me on the right track.

It was—still is—mind boggling how much information I found on forgiveness. The importance of forgiveness. The impact of forgiveness. My mind was blown, but I needed to know how to forgive effectively. It worried me. *Is there a right way to do it? What if I mess up? What if it doesn't work? What if it can't help me move forward after all?* It was scary, but I was determined to at least give it a shot. What did I have to lose? Nothing!

One day, finally, I felt I was ready to forgive my mother. In my head I started a conversation with her, and I said out loud: "I forgive you for everything you put me through, for all the hurt you inflicted, and for making it clear you never wanted or loved me."

It felt so good as the weight lifted off my shoulders and out of my heart. It was the beginning of my journey of true forgiveness.

Saying the words out loud was a relief. I felt wonderful afterward. I honestly felt that I had forgiven her and could move forward.

Turns out, it was only the first step. Although it was a huge step, it was only the beginning of my freedom from her. The first step on the journey of forgiveness is the *willingness* to forgive. It is an important step, but certainly not the only one, as I soon learned.

I realized I had more work to do in this department when I still got angry and uneasy any time I talked about what my mother had done to me. She still had power over me. How could this be? By forgiving, was I not taking back my power?

Over time I learned that forgiveness must come from a place of love. Despite my intentions, I had to find a way to love her and what she did to me, to accept what happened and take ownership of it all. I am not saying we need to accept blame. But we do need to take ownership. Ownership of our feelings, our reactions, our mindset.

So much easier said than done! It requires pushing through all the anger, frustrations, and emotions and embracing it all. It's hard work, but there is no way around it. It doesn't happen overnight—in fact, it can take a long time. It is painful, and there are times when it feels hopeless. Don't give up! Stay the course and work on it diligently.

If you can't do it on your own, do what I did: get some help. There is no shame in admitting you can't do it alone. Reach out for guidance, and don't give up when it gets difficult and overwhelming.

It took me a few years to truly forgive my mother. Many times I was convinced I had forgiven her for sure this time.

Nope, remnants of anger and blame lingered and held on. Each time her name was mentioned, or when people asked if I had heard anything from her, or when I came across old photographs, I felt my own nagging anger still hanging on.

Why? I think I wasn't yet ready to take full ownership. It still hurt, and I still felt like the little girl who so desperately wanted her mother's love and acceptance. Until I was ready to let go of this powerless little girl, I was trapped and unable to forgive and move forward.

One day it clicked. I have no magic wand or formula to give you. Your journey is to work through it for yourself in a manner and timeframe that works for you.

A few years ago, I finally released it all and took ownership. Piece by piece, feeling by feeling, emotion by emotion, I addressed each piece as it came up. Maybe you can address things faster or in bulk. Everybody is different, and we need to do what works for us.

As I peeled back the layers of my onion, exposed one issue after the other, and confronted and dealt with each one, my life felt lighter and I was happier. Releasing each thing loosened my shackles little by little and allowed happiness into my soul. It was a tough and painful journey, but so very worth it.

When I started my work on forgiveness, I thought I had to actually tell my mother that I forgive her. Imagine my relief when I learned I didn't have to do this at all! But if I don't actually tell her I forgive her, how will she know? Don't I have to tell her in order for it to be real and effective?

When I discovered she doesn't need to be a physical, in-person part of the whole exercise, I sighed with relief. If it seems counterintuitive to you, no worries, I was confused as well. Part of my blockage to completely forgive her had been my fear of having to confront her. I didn't want to interact with her, as I knew I would feel intimidated and I'd become that scared little girl in an instant.

Forgiveness is not about telling someone you forgive them. Forgiveness is all about you, and it frees you to move on. Forgiveness releases the claws holding you back and down. The surprising truth is that those claws belong to you.

Forgiving others really consists of forgiving ourselves for *blaming* others. When we blame others for our unhappiness, we give up our power, and that adds weight to our burden of unhappiness. By forgiving myself, I take back my power.

Once I take back my power, the other person is automatically released from blame—they are forgiven.

Forgiveness comes from deep inside of us. Once we have truly forgiven, we can move forward in freedom. Once we have truly forgiven, we can see the story as if it happened to somebody else. Once we have truly forgiven, we can talk about the things that transpired without all the feelings of pain, anger, and hopelessness. Once we have truly forgiven, we can live life without that dark cloud hanging overhead.

Forgiveness comes from love and compassion. My mother passed away a few years ago, and we never mended fences in person. Matter of fact, the last time I saw her, I told her to never contact me or my family again. I was done. I was able to tell her to her face without all the emotions of anger and hate. At that point I had already forgiven her. The forgiveness was not for her, but for me. I forgave her not to her face, but from my heart.

Do I hate my mother? There is no point. In my journey to forgive, I learned to love her and be grateful for her, for she gave me life and didn't kill me. I learned to love the lessons she taught me. You can choose to love somebody, but that does not mean you have to like them or to have them in your life.

My mother had a crappy life and made choices that didn't enhance her life, her personality, or her relationships. It was her life, and she chose how she wanted to live it. It's okay.

There will always be people or circumstances that make us hurt and make life difficult. Stuff happens—to everybody. Forgive. Forgive yourself for blaming the people and the circumstances. Most of the time we don't know why people are how they are or do what they do. It's their story, and we are merely a little part of that story. Don't let that incident in their life take over your life. Acknowledge it, forgive yourself for carrying any blame or resentment, and in doing so you forgive them. Learn from it and move on.

People are not always aware when they have hurt you. They have been on their own rough road and may not yet have learned to forgive themselves. Be compassionate toward them. Let them know that you care and that there is hope.

To forgive others, forgive yourself! Forgive your flaws and your perfect imperfections. Look in the mirror and say, *"Your Name,* I forgive you for...."

Do this for each and every thing you want to forgive yourself for. Do it daily for thirty days.

"Forgiveness is not always easy. At times, it feels more painful than the wound we suffered, to forgive the one that inflicted it. And yet, there is no peace without forgiveness."
Marianne Williamson

Notes and Thoughts

For what will you forgive yourself today?

Step 3: **Love Yourself**

"Love who you are, embrace who you are. Love yourself. When you love yourself, people can kind of pick up on that: they can see confidence, they can see self-esteem, and naturally, people gravitate towards you."
Lilly Singh

love
noun – love /ləv/
- strong affection for another arising out of kinship or personal ties

It saddens me that the dictionary definition of love is about love for others or things. Don't get me wrong, it is great to love and be loved. It is a wonderful feeling. But how can we love somebody else if we don't love ourselves first?

To love, accept, and respect yourself is the greatest gift you can give yourself. It is one of the most important gifts not only to yourself but to those around you. And no, it is not at all selfish. It is critical.

It would be selfish if we loved ourselves only to reap personal gain from all of our interactions. That's what it means to be self-absorbed, and rarely are self-absorbed folks happy.

The self-love I am talking about is love for yourself that makes you flourish. When you look in the mirror, do you like what you see? Not just on the outside but also on the inside? When you look at yourself, can you smile and say, "I love you unconditionally"?

Can you look at yourself and accept your blemishes and flaws? Who says they are blemishes or flaws anyway? Is society whispering in your ear, saying you are not pretty enough? Not successful enough? Not good enough? Who defines these absurd standards, anyway? It must be folks who neither love nor like themselves.

Why do we judge ourselves and others by ridiculous exterior standards? Is it because we see those standards superimposed to create images of beauty and success? Most commercial photos of beautiful people are "Photoshopped" to enhance cheekbones or trim underarm fat or erase wrinkles. Real life cannot be Photoshopped. Our solution is to appreciate who we are and what we see.

We grow up comparing ourselves to others and working hard to fit into a mental image influenced by complete strangers. We try desperately to measure up. We do what is expected from our parents, teachers, peers, employers, friends, etc. We enter the rat race in search of beauty and success but end up losing ourselves and, thereby, our happiness.

Humans need love to survive and flourish. We all want to be loved and accepted, and we strive to find it anywhere we can. Mostly we look to receive love from others.

Why do we look for it from others? We cannot love and accept others if we don't first love and accept ourselves. How can we give if our cup is empty?

Do we need permission to love ourselves without feeling guilty? I did, and it took a long time before I realized it was not only okay, but necessary to love myself. I gave myself permission. Give yourself permission now if you have not done so yet. Permission can come from no one but you.

In my struggle to overcome obstacles, the side effects were destruction of self-esteem and lack of self-love. After all, my own mother couldn't or wouldn't love me. Therefore, I must be an awful human being. Something must be wrong with me.

Each time I looked in the mirror, I saw a fat, ugly blob staring back at me. An unlovable, unworthy human being. It hurt to see my classmates smiling and happy with their loving families. I was envious and resentful—envious for what they had and I lacked; resentful because I felt I could never have it.

Growing up longing to be loved and accepted made me vulnerable to all sorts of predators, even long into adulthood. I welcomed with open arms anybody who showed me kindness. More times than not, I was blindsided and taken advantage of. Fortunately, my guardian angels protected me from extreme physical danger.

Food was my friend. It comforted me and never judged. It hugged me when I was physically and emotionally hurting. It kept me company when I was all alone, bored, and wallowing in self-pity. Though food provided temporary comfort, it also made me resentful toward myself as I piled on the pounds. Inside I felt I would never be happy, never love or be loved, never be pretty or smart. It was an emotional roller-coaster.

I went from anger, to frustration, to hate, to despair, to grief, to hope (fortunately, I always managed to have some hope), and back to frustration. The cycle continued for too long. I cried enough tears to contribute greatly to the ocean. I wept to let it all out in hopes I would feel better.

Because I didn't know how to love myself, my self-worth and self-esteem were non-existent. The hopelessness was so vast, I felt I couldn't escape. Every once in a while, I'd see a little glimmer of light, of hope. A kind word from my mother. An embrace. Maybe she does love me after all and I am worth it! Do I dare to hope and cling to that dream?

Too many times my little flame of hope was snuffed out before it could grow into a beautiful, all-illuminating flame. Back I fell, into the darkness of my abyss. Back to the negative self-talk and self-hate.

Fortunately, some people showed me kindness and compassion. They fanned that little spark of hope and love. They taught me to love myself. They showed me I was worthy. I began to cling to them. Yes, I had a tendency to cling to anyone who showed me kindness and compassion.

Piece by piece and little by little, I learned to love and honor myself. I suffered setbacks, but I always managed to pull myself back up and out of the abyss. Climbing out became easier and easier.

The struggles and setbacks were daunting. At times I felt I had moved three steps ahead, only to fall back four or five steps. The fact that I carried over 350 pounds on a 5'6" frame did not help. I saw how people looked at me and whispered behind my back. Maybe they were right. Maybe I didn't deserve to be happy and loved.

WRONG!!!

We all deserve to be happy and to be loved! Something had to change! I had to change. My self-talk had to change. I had two young boys and a loving husband. Because I didn't like myself and couldn't love myself, I was subconsciously pushing them away and keeping them at arm's length.

One day in early 2004, I was at my breaking point. The physical and emotional pain was incredible and overwhelming. How could I move on? This was my darkest hour—and also my turning point. You see, I was contemplating suicide. End it all. Be done. The end.

But I discovered that, even though I had no self-esteem, self-worth, or self-love, I was not a quitter! I thought of the people who were most important to me. My kids needed their mom. My amazing husband needed his wife to help raise these incredible young men. Checking out was not an option!

That insight was my turning point. That day I took charge of my well-being and my happiness. I started by writing in my gratitude journal, doing the exercise from Step 1 in this book. That is when I started practicing gratitude.

That spring I enrolled into college classes. *Nobody will be able to say I am stupid if I have a degree!* Later that year, I underwent gastric bypass surgery, and it was do or die at that point. Those were the beginning steps of claiming and loving myself.

I lost weight; I passed my classes with 3.5 grade point averages and above; my physical pain diminished. With that, the dark clouds in my mind began to lift. Very slowly I gained self-esteem and self-worth. I started to love myself, and as time went by, I even started to like myself.

The conversations I had with myself became less self-sabotaging and less self-destructive. My self-respect grew, and I gained more and more confidence. I began to shift from within.

Don't get me wrong, it wasn't all sunshine and rainbows. There were still storms to weather, but they became fewer and fewer and less frequent. Sunshine was becoming my new norm. And somewhere along the way, I learned to dance in the rain.

As I talked to myself with more kindness, love, and respect, my confidence grew. Looking in the mirror was no longer horrifying. I started to like what I saw. There was a kind, beautiful, loving, caring person emerging, ready to take her place in the world. She was ready to come out from the shadows and claim her spot in the light.

Do you read personal development books? Do you watch motivational speakers on YouTube or go see them at live events? The energy at a live event will sweep you away and energize you like there is no tomorrow!

I started reading books by John Maxwell, Jack Canfield, and Dale Carnegie, to name a few. Whenever possible, I went to live events with great speakers like Tony Robbins, Lisa Nichols, and Zig Ziglar. While driving, I listened to Jim Rohn, Joe Vitale, and so many more. They whispered in my ear and inspired me. They became my mentors and coaches.

Who do you listen to when you are driving? Whose books are you reading to help you along your journey? Listen to people who inspire you, and they don't have to be famous. Listen to a teacher, professor, friend, family member, or neighbor. I have found I can learn from everyone I encounter.

I found it interesting that, as I grew and evolved, those who had been my "friends" when I was miserable, overweight, and down in the dumps, disappeared into thin air. All of a sudden, they were avoiding me, not inviting me to get-togethers. And suddenly, folks who previously wouldn't give me the time of day now approached me to strike up conversations.

What was happening? It was a strange sensation to be shunned by those who had been my friends when I was down and welcomed by those who didn't see me when I was in the abyss. It took me some time to figure it out, but eventually I did.

You see, as I lost the weight, took more classes, and changed my overall attitude and outlook, my vibration changed. Apparently there's truth to the saying, "Your vibe attracts your tribe." As I changed and evolved, so did the company I kept. It is still happening to this day, and I am loving it.

I have often wondered if my breakthrough would have come sooner if I had been more selective of the company I keep. Jim Rohn said that we are the average of the five people we spend the most time with. Boy was he right! Now I could see it clear as day!

At first, I beat myself up over losing old friends. The self-doubts kept creeping back, until I realized the reason those friends didn't stick around was simply because I was evolving.

My self-talk became more positive and supportive instead of negative and derogatory. My internal voices cheered me on, encouraging me to move forward, try new things, and—dare I say it—love me!

Now I am completely okay with who I am, where I am in life, and what I want. No longer am I afraid to be alone with myself. No longer do I need constant background stimulation to drown out my own voice and thoughts. I like who I have become, and I love me—faults, blemishes, extra pounds, loose skin, and all.

My relationship with my husband and sons is better than ever. The sun seems to shine brighter, and even the storms have a strange, awesome beauty about them.

Be aware that every day is a new adventure and an opportunity to grow as a person. It's a chance to be happier and love more than you did the day before. It's a new time to fall in love with yourself all over again.

Love yourself. Embrace yourself. Like and cherish every perfect imperfection. You are unique. You are amazing. You are incredible. Celebrate you in each and every moment. Tell yourself all the wonderful and encouraging things you would tell your children to make them feel safe, loved, wanted, and cherished.

It has to start with you. You cannot pour from an empty cup. Only when your cup is full can you share with an open heart. You are the most important person in your life. You are the gift of love for others.

Only when our hearts are full and we can love and appreciate ourselves, can we give unconditional love.

Speak kindly to yourself. Show yourself the love and compassion you so freely give to others. You are a perfectly imperfect creation and so richly deserve the very best the Universe has to offer.

Surround yourself with people who uplift and build you up. The company you keep makes a huge difference. Positive words, experiences, and people will raise your happy vibration. Everything is energy, and energy attracts more energy like itself. Vibrate at a higher lever to attract better things, people, and circumstances for yourself.

Your vibe attracts your tribe!

Love yourself so you can love others. Be kind to yourself so you can be kind to others. Accept yourself so you can accept others.

Not sure where to start? Write a love letter to yourself. Leave little love notes for yourself. Pay attention to your self-talk. Treat yourself to a manicure, pedicure, dinner at a fancy restaurant, a massage, a personal trainer, flowers, or whatever will make you feel appreciation and love.

It may sound silly, but it works. Try it. When was the last time you did something just for you?

Do the same exercise with love as you did for forgiveness, only this time look in the mirror and say, "*Your Name,* I love and appreciate you for...."

Do this for each and every thing you love and appreciate about yourself. Do it daily for thirty days.

"*I think the most important thing in life is self-love, because if you don't have self-love and respect for everything about your own body, your own soul, your own capsule, then how can you have an authentic relationship with anyone else?*"

Shailene Woodley

Notes and Thoughts

What do you like and love about yourself?

Step 4: **Nurture the Subconscious**

"The happiness of your life depends upon the quality of your thoughts...."

Marcus Aurelius

subconscious
noun - sub·con·scious /səbˈkänSHəs/
- existing in the mind but not immediately to consciousness

Wise words from Marcus Aurelius. What we let into our subconscious is more important than you might think. Our subconscious functions on a simple, unemotional, matter-of-fact level. It takes everything we dump into it at face value and then sets into motion events and experiences to validate our beliefs and desires.

Our subconscious is like a child. It starts as a blank slate and collects all of our incoming information. Or compare it to a garden with empty beds ready to be filled and planted.

Countless studies have been conducted on the conscious and subconscious mind. No worries, I won't bore you with technical terms and findings. It is too overwhelming. One commonalty seems to be that our subconscious sets into motion what our conscious mind commands.

The subconscious mind is like fertile garden soil, ready to produce flowers, fruits, vegetables, and weeds. You, the conscious mind, are the gardener. You decide what to grow, select the plants you want, settle them into the soil, and envision the bountiful harvest.

We all do it. We plant the seed and then dream about the outcome. We imagine the delicious foods we will prepare, the gorgeous flowers we will bring into the house to fill the air with their beautiful fragrance. Can you smell and taste them?

But before we can enjoy the bounty, we must tend the garden. We need to fertilize, water, pull the weeds, etc. We have to do this consistently while our garden slowly grows. We have to give it the best care for maximum results. We have to work together with our garden.

We can also train the plants to grow in a certain way. Think of a bonsai tree. It is cared for and trimmed in a very specific way to grow into the beautiful form we create. We can also purchase lucky bamboo plants that have been woven into lovely patterns (a heart, a waffle, a spiral, etc.). To achieve the desired shape, the gardener must repeatedly perform the same act of positioning, cutting, and directing the growth.

Our conscious and subconscious essentially work in that same way. Our conscious mind is the gardener tending to the subconscious, the soil. When we are born, the fertile soil of our empty garden is ready to receive. The plants are our thoughts and words. Everything we ever hear, experience, feel, or encounter is recorded, stored, and "planted," even things we don't desire to harvest. Our mind receives thoughts and ideas and beliefs from others, like seeds blown in on the wind. The roots are the neural pathways that grow and connect in our brain. The more frequently we use a mental path, the more established and easier it is to access.

The more accustomed we are to certain thoughts, words, and feelings, the easier they are for us to use. Our subconscious learns the pattern, and because it becomes familiar, it brings a feeling of comfort, letting us know all is okay.

When the subconscious cannot find a pattern for new incoming information, it reacts with discomfort. We feel fear, anxiety, uneasiness, depression, and so forth. Our subconscious signals us to stop this behavior and go back to what we know and what is comfortable. In a dangerous situation, it might signal us to run away quickly.

The job of our subconscious is to protect us and follow the orders we give it through our conscious thoughts and words. It is our army, and we are the commanding general. It is ready to do our bidding. Pretty powerful, wouldn't you say?

Here is where we, from our conscious mind, play a huge part in how our life plays out. We get bombarded with information and data all day long—through TV, radio, social media, our thoughts, our conversations, and the conversations we overhear. We have constant input to attend to.

Like the random seeds blown into our garden by the wind, a lot of what enters our subconscious is undesired weeds and pollution. It is negative. Sometimes we throw good and positive info into the mix, but so much is negative.

Some of the seeds blown in by the wind will be beautiful flowers or nourishing fruits or vegetables, some will be weeds. If we don't tend to the sprouting seeds in the garden of our mind, the weeds of negativity will take over and choke out the luscious fruits, vegetables, and flowers we desire. Positivity might grow for a little while, but a continual onslaught of negativity will cause the positive to wither away.

As I grew up in Germany (not a happy upbringing), I felt my English was not good. Even though English was taught in school, proper Oxford English and spoken American English might as well be classified as separate languages.

The night I met my husband, I had been partying with friends, and the alcohol had relaxed my self-doubts. In my relaxed state, my English was fantastic, and we had a great conversation. The next day was a different story. My side of the conversation was comprised of one-syllable words and short, clipped sentences.

I was very much smitten with this handsome young soldier and wanted to continue the relationship. But due to the language barrier, I was worried it might not happen. Don't get me wrong, I knew the vocabulary and the sentence structures. That wasn't the issue.

The issue was, I was horrified that what I wanted to say would come out wrong. I was terrified of using the wrong words and sounding like a fool. In my head, I laid out the sentences in German and translated them into English before I would utter them. As you can imagine, those were slow, painful conversations, at least from where I was sitting.

The point is I was very uncomfortable, and my subconscious aimed to play it safe by trying to keep me quiet. Those who know me know that's not an easy feat. If I had let my subconscious guide me and played it safe, chances are my husband and I would not be together today.

I fell head over heels for this guy. It was a feeling I never thought possible. With every fiber in my body I knew he was the ONE. But there was that language barrier. Could I overcome it? Clearly, I must have, since we have been married for almost thirty years now.

What did I do? I changed the way I approached the situation. In case you are wondering, I did not stay intoxicated until I got it right. What I did was, instead of letting the fear take over and curling up in safety by looking for a German guy, I learned the English of the man who captured my heart.

Oh, it was so very uncomfortable for quite some time! We watched movies, and I understood maybe a word here and there. Some movies I had seen in German, so I was familiar with them. Most were new to me. After a while, I understood the context of the movie. Why? Because I consciously nourished my new pathways (the flowers I wanted to harvest). I tended to them diligently daily, pulling the weeds, watering, trimming, fertilizing, etc.

Our conversations got longer and better. Before long, I was able to understand it all—TV shows, movies, other Americans. I felt victorious. It was short-lived, as my husband was deployed with his unit to serve in Desert Storm. Did you know news English is different from regular, everyday English? Neither did I!

Predictably, my beautiful garden encountered another set of weeds. I must have become a good gardener, because I figured out the "newscast" English very quickly. Although I was born and raised in Germany and German was the first language I learned, English has been my primary language for almost as long as we have been together.

Can you see where I am going with this? In the beginning, I had to speak English on a very conscious level. Each word was thought out and planned, since I had to get it right in order for my husband to understand me. It was tough and very uncomfortable.

Now, English is natural to me. It's almost as if it is the only language I ever learned. It is as easy as breathing, and it happens on the subconscious level. No longer do I need to formulate the sentence in German and then translate in my head before speaking the words. English is now my comfort zone.

In my subconscious garden, I tended to and nourished my English "flowers" with English fertilizer and English care, whatever it took to flourish. Fun fact: English has become so natural to me that I failed the German part of a test to become a translator! If somebody had told me in high school that this would happen, I'd have died laughing!

What does all this have to do with the conscious, subconscious and happiness? Simple. The thoughts you feed, tend to, and nourish will grow and flourish.

Do you pay attention to your thoughts and the words you speak? Do you communicate with yourself and others intentionally, or is your communication more automatic?

Do you pay attention to what you let enter your mind and, therefore, your subconscious? What pathways do you nourish? Do you give your attention to the flowers, fruits, and vegetables, or do you succumb to the weeds? When you listen to the chatter in your head—your self-talk—is it negative or positive? When you notice your thoughts, are they positive or negative? The more negative you let in, the more negative your thoughts and self-talk will be, and the more negative experiences you will have.

Negative thinking can take over your experience like weeds take over a beautiful garden. Repeated negative thoughts can smother your positive dreams and desires. A huge, weed-filled garden feels utterly overwhelming and daunting. When weedy, negative thinking becomes the norm, it paralyzes positive growth and experience.

Does the avid gardener abandon his garden? No, he pulls out the weeds one by one. He gets to work and finishes the job no matter what, because he knows all that he planted is still there under all the weeds. The fresh sprouts might not be visible under the canopy of weeds, but he knows they are still there.

He knows that if he pulls all the weeds, fertilizes, and waters the soil, everything he planted will return better and stronger than ever.

Once upon a time, there was a Cherokee grandfather who told his grandson, "Grandson, there are two wolves inside of me. One wolf is white, good, and altruistic, generous and kind, and the other wolf is black, mean, and greedy, violent and angry. The two wolves are in a constant fight within me." The grandson, with wide eyes, said, "But which one will win, Grandpa?" And the grandfather said "The one which I feed."

The wolves within you are the positive and negative influences in your subconscious. Do you feed and nurture the negative because it is what you know and what you are bombarded with 24/7 in your surroundings? Or do you keep the negative out by focusing only on positive thoughts, words, and images?

It takes practice and mindfulness to flip the switch of habitual thinking. It can be uncomfortable at first. There will be challenges, and you might slip back into the old pattern. No worries. As soon as you catch yourself, get back on track of positive focus. The more you use your new neural pathways, the more comfortable they become. Soon you will be astounded by how automatic it feels to focus in this new way.

Pay attention to what you let into your subconscious. Your subconscious is here to deliver what you put your attention on. Remember, the subconscious does not question your commands, it has no sense of humor, and it is here to comply. It's only black and white. It is your conscious mind that adds the color and the humor and gives the command.

I believe the subconscious conspires with the Universe and its laws to create the life we want, and numerous authors and philosophers back me up: James Allen (*As a Man Thinketh*); Napoleon Hill (*Think and Grow Rich*). One of my favorite sayings is, "What you think about you bring about."

Do you know the subconscious does not compute *no, don't,* or *won't*? Strange, isn't it? When we think, "I don't want that to happen to me," our subconscious hears, "I want that to happen," and it starts working to make it happen. Focus on the positive opposite outcome of the situation you do want. Better thoughts, better outcome.

What helped me shift my thoughts and pay attention to what I let into my subconscious was, and still is, a ten-day mental diet. When we are on a diet, we pay more attention to what we put into our bodies. The same principal works with the mental diet. I am currently in year ... I have no clue.

How can I be in year X in a program that is only ten days? Simple. In this diet, you cannot have any negative thoughts or words for ten consecutive days. As soon as you catch yourself, you have to re-focus the negative to a positive and—you guessed it—your diet starts over. Example: you are driving on the highway and that one person cuts you off. You get mad at that driver. Stop. Redirect and focus on all the other drivers who didn't cut you off and be grateful for them. And the diet starts over.

This has helped me pay attention to my thoughts and words. Those negative ones still sneak in, but they happen much less frequently, and I catch them super quickly and immediately redirect.

This practice has helped me be more relaxed, less fearful, more grateful, less angry, and yes, a lot happier.

Consciously bring in good, positive thoughts. Nourish your newly forming neural pathways and make them your new superhighways. Be mindful of what you let slip into your subconscious. "Garbage in garbage out." Value in value out.

"Whatever we plant in our subconscious mind and nourish with repetition and emotion will one day become a reality."
Earl Nightingale

Notes and Thoughts

What have you been letting into your subconscious? What do you want to invite into your subconscious?

Step 5: **Mindset**

"Resolutions are a wonderful thing if we can keep them, but many resolutions go by the wayside because we have not done anything different with our mindset."

Monica Johnson

mindset
Noun – mindset / 'mīn(d)set
- a mental attitude or inclination
- a fixed state of mind

Take this simple test: Imagine you are to ask your boss for a raise. You know you have been working your tail off and you are a great employee. You might imagine several scenarios. Go ahead, play them all out in your head. If you are an entrepreneur, you can play out the scenario with a big client you are trying to win, or role-play any other conversation you need to have.

Did you, like most, play out the worst-case scenarios? Did you imagine you had to argue and counterargue? In your role-play, did you get the result you wanted? How did you feel?

Now, play out the same conversation, except this time take the opposite approach. Instead of the whole thing going south and your blood pressure going up in frustration, imagine everything works out exactly as you want it to.

What do you feel now? Are you more confident, lighter, and happier? The effort was exactly the same! If it was harder to imagine everything going right, it may be because you are programmed to automatically imagine the worst-case scenario. It is easier to take the negative route when that is how our neural pathways are conditioned and trained.

Imagining the positive outcome, for most humans, is the road less traveled. The positive pathway might be barely visible, but it is there. Positive thinking and a positive outlook on life is a mindset. Its negative counterpart is also a mindset. Remember, what you let into your subconscious and what you nourish will grow. The more you nurture it, the more it will become the first thing you access, because you have made it familiar. It feels safe and comfortable.

Have you ever known someone who is complacent and convinced that this is as good as it will ever get? *It has been like this for generations. It's just the way it is. Might as well get used to it.*

Why? Is it because we have stopped dreaming? What happened to the daydreams of your childhood? Have they been squished by well-meaning adults who wanted to prepare you for "real" life? Perhaps their dreams had been squished early on as well.

It takes energy, effort, and determination to swim against the current. Grown-ups have wisdom and knowledge, and we are told we should listen to their teachings. We are "only kids," and we need to obey and respect our elders and teachers.

We don't know what dreams and aspirations they gave up on. Maybe they wanted to be an astronaut, a doctor, a gymnast, a firefighter, a clown, an artist, or a writer, but someone snuffed out their dream, told them to be practical and realistic.

And that is what they pass on to us. But what does that even mean? Little by little, our dreams and hopes were diminished and stomped on until we gave up on them and conformed.

Our mind, once open and free to think and imagine, has been boxed up and sealed. We entered the group-think mindset. Know anyone on this wavelength? *Money is tight. We can't afford it. Go to school and get good grades so you can get into a good college and get a good job. Our family* has a long line of teachers, military, academics, etc. *so we expect you go the same route.* Sound familiar?

As I was raised in Germany by a single mom, money was tight. There were times I wasn't sure whether I would eat or not. A lot of my clothes came from the social services donation bin. Every time I asked for things I needed or wanted, I was told we had no money, or, "Why don't you get a job so you can contribute and buy what you need?"

From an early age it was drilled into me that there is not enough to go around. There were rich people and there were us. We scraped by. Even when I had money from walking dogs or other odd jobs, I was forbidden to spend it, required to save it. *You never know when an emergency might strike.*

I dreaded going to get clothes from the social services donation bin. Every fiber in my body screamed and hoped something would happen to keep us from going. Every time I wished very hard that no clothes would be available. But every time, the bin was full—full with outdated, worn-out clothes others deemed not worth wearing. But we had no money, and free was "good."

Interestingly, the funding shortage only seemed to apply to me. My mother always had money to shop for new outfits for herself or anything she wanted. I didn't realize this until much later.

So, here I was with "new" clothes to wear to school. I was mortified! Kids can be so cruel. I remember going to school one day in a mustard, poop-colored plaid outfit that made me itch all over my body. There was no hole I could crawl into—and believe me, I looked.

On my long walk to school, I considered ditching class in order to avoid being ridiculed. The idea was short-lived, as I knew the beating I would receive if my mother found out. My self-esteem sank even lower. I went to school and hoped nobody would notice me or pay attention to me.

No such luck. All morning, kids called me names and made fun of me, even more than usual. One person called me a "poor mouse looking for scraps." Something inside me gave up. At that moment, I believed I was a poor, good-for-nothing, scavenger.

I succumbed to my existence and circumstances. My mindset had become that of a poverty-stricken, desperate, and hopeless person. I was convinced there would never be enough, and I would always live in the bottom section of society.

Fortunately, I moved on to go to boarding school. It was a private, co-ed school in a beautiful old abbey nestled in a corner where two valleys meet. My mother couldn't afford to send me there, but child social services in Stuttgart made it possible.

Some of the kids who attended my school had parents who paid their tuition. To me, those families were like royalty, and I thought they must be the richest people in the world. As you can imagine, I had a hard time fitting in. I always felt like an outsider with my nose pressed to the window. Close enough to see, but too far to ever touch.

At least now I could get new clothes twice a year through social services. All I had to do is write out a list of what and how much I needed: three pairs of jeans, five T-shirts, three blouses, socks, underwear, and whatever else I could think of. They provided me with the money to purchase WHAT I WANTED.

Still, I was hesitant to spend all the money. *What if there is an emergency and I need something?* Often I didn't buy what I really wanted or needed, because I felt guilty spending the money.

I went to work at a factory over summer break to make extra money for the year. There was usually one "big" thing I splurged on with my earnings. One year I bought a bicycle to have at boarding school. It was a proud moment, and yet I felt guilty for having spent all that money on a bicycle for myself.

Some of my friends seemed to be so careless about money. It seemed they never cared what they purchased or what they spent it on. Those were the popular kids. I was never popular. They were rich. I was poor. In my mind, there was a direct relation between financial worth and popularity or happiness.

The years went by, but my core beliefs about money hadn't changed. I never seemed to have enough to do what I wanted to do or buy what I wanted to buy. Often times I didn't even have enough to purchase what I needed.

I felt there was never enough of anything. Not enough love. Not enough money. Not enough food. Not enough clothes. Not enough of anything. Ever.

This belief instilled in me a mindset of scarcity. Certainly happiness was scarce. "You need money to be happy." That's the message I received growing up. If you don't have money, you don't have friends, because you can't keep up with them. Without money, you cannot be a part of a better class of people. Without money, you are stuck where you are physically, mentally, and emotionally.

I felt inferior around my friends. Each time I connected with them, my self-esteem shrunk a little more. I convinced myself that I would never amount to anything, that I would never be good enough, that there was not enough to go around. Only the rich can have the good life. How sad that made me!

What we feed our mind and reinforce has a powerful effect on our experience. We sometimes do it so automatically, we are not even aware it is happening. The stigma we grow up with is ingrained deep within our mind. As I said before, the conscious feeds the subconscious mind. What we take in and focus on becomes our mindset.

Because we didn't have money growing up, I believed things like:
- Money is the root of all evil.
- There is never enough; there will never be enough.
- Money is for somebody else, but not for us.
- I don't measure up.
- I am not good enough.

- I don't deserve.
- Things only work for others.
- Money is not that important. It's only money.
- The rich get richer and the poor get poorer.
- Our family has never been rich.
- You can either be rich or happy, but not both.
- Life is hard.

Do some of those statements sound familiar to you? Have you heard them repeatedly as you grew up? Do you still play those tapes in your head? I certainly have, and every so often, when I don't pay attention to my thoughts, I still catch one of those tunes playing clearly. The programming is hardcore. This conditioned mindset lasts a very, very long time, and we need to break the habit.

But old habits are hard to break. That's another limiting belief. Stop it! The "not enough" mindset is simply a limiting belief engrained and affirmed over and over. The "not enough" and overall negative mindset has built the biggest neural superhighways in the history of highways.

We keep it going and well maintained by running the scarcity, limiting beliefs, and negative talk tape over and over. Fixing a pothole here, fixing a pothole there. Enforcing the pillars holding it up. Paving and repaving the road to make sure all runs smoothly.

Stop it. Stop playing the victim. Just stop it.

Take the exit and get off.

It is time to take the road less traveled and to travel it over and over again until it is deeply carved. Revisit those new thought patterns. Pave the way for a mindset of abundance and positivity, a mindset of knowing there is always enough for everybody and it will be all right.

Build that superhighway little by little, new thought and belief by new thought and belief. Just like a dirt path becomes smoother and easier to travel the more it is used, practicing this new thinking will make it easier for you to access the mindset of plenty, love, positivity, and happiness.

It takes some work. You have to be deliberate and on purpose. It is like learning how to ride a bike. Do you remember how scared you were the first time you got on your bike? Did you have training wheels to keep you steady? Did you have a parent hold on to your saddle as you pedaled on so you wouldn't fall?

Creating new neural pathways, thought patterns, and mindset is like learning to ride a bike. First, you have to want it. You have to want it so badly that you will do whatever it takes to learn. As with riding a bike, there will be some setbacks: falls, cuts, and bruises. It doesn't matter. They will heal, and you will find your balance and fall less often.

Imagine teaching a baby to walk. The baby pulls himself to standing, holding on to a couch or table or parent's hand and takes his first wobbly step. He falls, gets up, tries again. Falls, gets up, and manages to take two steps before falling again. The parent cheers him on. He gets up and tries over and over. Before long, he goes from stumbling and falling to running without even tripping.

Be the parent for your mindset. Cheer yourself on. Celebrate your smallest victories. Keep pushing forward and the small victories will become bigger and better. Keep cheering for yourself.

How can you change a mindset from negative and poverty stricken to positive and full of abundance? It is easier than you might think. It takes some conscious effort and requires some work, but no worries. There's no heavy lifting.

Start the exercises from these chapters: the gratitude journal, the ten-day mental diet, the forgiveness and love-yourself exercises. These will accustom your mind to a positive focus.

Over time, your subconscious will default to the positive route instead of the negative. As you become more conscious of your thoughts and keep them more positive, it will be easier and easier.

What does this poverty and abundance mindset have to do with happiness? Simple. As your thoughts about money are a mindset, so are your thoughts about happiness.

Happiness is a frame of mind. It's a choice we each can make. We can choose to be happy or not. Each morning I make the decision to be happy. It's my mindset, simple as that. After I practiced the mental exercises for some time, my happy meter rose along with my new positive thinking and self-talk. The sun now seems brighter, the sky bluer, and people are nicer and friendlier.

As your mindset changes, your happy meter will rise, and the new vibration you emit will attract better things, people, and circumstances into your experience.

Be mindful of your thoughts, as thoughts become things. Keep them positive, and before you know it, you will have a brand new, happier mindset.

"You're braver than you believe, stronger than you seem, and smarter than you think."
Winnie the Pooh

Notes and Thoughts

What are some of your core beliefs? What new core beliefs do you want to carve for yourself?

Step 6: **Go with the Flow**

"I equate ego with trying to figure everything out instead of going with the flow. That closes your heart and your mind to the person or situation that's right in front of you, and you miss so much."
Pema Chodron

Go with the Flow
Phrase
- to do what seems like the easiest thing in a particular situation

Going with the flow in the context of finding your happiness does not mean to become a follower and participate in every new fad and trend. I am not saying don't do that—by all means, if that adds to your happiness, go for it.

The flow I am talking about is your life and energy flow. Are you mostly struggling, or do things come effortlessly for you? Do you feel as if you are fighting uphill battles in your career and personal life, or does almost everything you touch "turn to gold"?

We all have times when things easily fall into place and other times not so much. Have you experienced periods everything was going well and more of the good stuff kept coming? Do you remember how good it felt? Then, suddenly, something happened and it came to a screeching halt, and everything started to unravel right before your eyes?

It happens to all of us. Energy flows continuously in a never-ending pattern like a river flowing in its bed. The individual water drop does not know where it is going, but it trusts the flow.

Our lives are like a river. There is the general direction from birth to death. A river starts at its headwaters, then flows to merge with another river or empties into an ocean or lake or eventually fizzles out and dries up.

The river finds the best route to travel, first as a little stream. The more water it contains, the more it chisels the ground to form its bed. It does not take a straight path but takes the path of least resistance.

It can take quite some time for a little stream to become a mighty river forging its way through the planet. The flow of the Colorado River carved out the Grand Canyon. Scientists estimate the Grand Canyon was formed four to six million years ago. Some argue it might have been seventy million years in the making.

At one point the Colorado River, instead of going around a rock formation, seemed to cut right through. It took time, but eventually the river forged the beautiful canyon that is one of the Seven Wonders of the World. It stayed its course and followed its flow.

The Colorado River did what it had to do and what came naturally to reach its destination. When it ran into obstacles, it found a new path. When it hit another snag, it found another route. It kept moving forward and carving its path wider and deeper.

Our lives are no different. From the time we are born we forge our life on the way to our final destination. We learn, implement, evaluate, learn more, implement more, and keep re-evaluating. Some things we learn work well for us; others not so much. We start out in one direction but end up changing course many times.

No matter if it is relationships, jobs, raising children, a career, or pursuing a hobby, some of it feels easy and natural, and some of it feels uncomfortable or nearly impossible.

Just as I tried to fit in growing up, I tried to find my path in life. Who am I? What do I want to do or be when I get older?

I struggled mightily as a grown-up trying to figure out this work situation. Clearly, as an adult I would need to do something to support myself. After I graduated with my *Abitur* (higher education entrance qualification) from boarding school, I figured I'd go to university. At the time, I thought I wanted to be a political journalist. No clue why, but I did. So, I registered for classes and started my first semester.

The first week was excruciating. The classrooms were overflowing (one of the side effects of free school), and unless I showed up thirty to sixty minutes before class, the only seats left were on the floor. Not what I had envisioned.

Nothing about college felt right at that time. What to do? Well, time to get a job. A friend helped me get hired at a factory. The work was monotonous and ever so boring. It paid the bills, but I wasn't happy.

I went on to different jobs, hoping with each one that it would be the "one." It didn't work out that way. Except for the years I stayed home to raise our boys, I jumped from job to job and opportunity to opportunity hoping each would be the one I could build my career on.

As a stay-at-home mom with time on her hands, I wanted to do something to contribute to our family's income. I became a Tupperware consultant, my first taste of entrepreneurship. It felt exciting—a new sensation for me while working.

We moved back to Germany, where I could not sell American Tupperware on post due to the SOFA (Status of Forces Agreement) between the US and Germany. What to do? That was an unexpected curve ball.

Since I couldn't work any U.S.- based MLM (Multi-Level Marketing/Network Marketing) business while overseas, I had to shift gears. My energy flow was disrupted, and I felt lost and a little defeated. Reset.

Instead of working, I started doing things for me, for my well-being. Yup, it coincided with the dark time I mentioned in Step 3. I was hungry to learn and ready to move forward. College was fun, and now my degree hangs over my desk like a trophy I earned for reclaiming my life.

An organization on post offered classes to help spouses understand the military lingo. I signed up, even though at that point I was already a seasoned military spouse. Eventually, I became a master trainer in the program. Sharing information with others felt good. Slowly, I could feel my energy flowing more smoothly again.

Eventually, we moved back to the States. The kids were now old enough not to need mom at home all the time. As I tried to figure out my next move, part of my issue was my identity. For so long I had been the wife, the mom, the army spouse. That was my flow, and it felt right.

However, something was nagging inside of me. My inner voice kept whispering, "There is more out there for you to do, to be." But what? Where would I begin? I thought it was time to build a career. I started by taking a job as a sales rep for a local newspaper, selling advertising spots. It didn't last.

From there, I found an administrative position with a contractor on our local military post. I felt more relaxed and comfortable in this position than I did in sales. It was interesting, and it landed me at the public affairs office. It was fun, challenging, and it flowed.

Since I was hired through a contractor, there was no guarantee the contract would be awarded again for the new fiscal year. So, I applied for a government position and started in the marketing department shortly thereafter.

Talk about bad energy flow! The job itself was no problem, but the supervisor was. Everything inside of me screamed to quit and walk away. The money was decent, and it helped us reach some goals, but I was miserable. My stress level went through the roof, and I could feel the darkness creeping back in. Nothing flowed with this position, and it affected all areas of my life and being. So, I quit.

Apparently, being an employee wasn't for me.

Sometime later, we moved to Colorado, and I started my business, Matters of Perspective. I had no clue what it would turn into, no clue what direction it would take. It felt good to have my own company, but it didn't pay the bills.

Network marketing came knocking again. In a seven-year period I had joined five or six different companies. I believed in the dream they were selling. I jumped in with both feet and struggled along, hoping to make it big with the next opportunity. Eventually, I realized network marketing is not for me. If it were, it wouldn't have been a constant struggle.

Not long ago, I faced yet another crossroads. I was over fifty years old and still had no acceptable career. I became a mortgage loan officer. It felt tangible, legitimate, and I could start quickly. I was excited about helping people with the biggest investment of their lives.

Again, nothing flowed. I struggled from day one. After one year on the struggle bus, I called it quits. Again.

But this time it was different. I had a different energy, a different feeling. For the first time ever, I didn't feel like a failure. Quitting this time felt right. I felt calm—something I had never experienced before.

You see, I had had one constant companion persistent in the background for decades. This companion showed up every time a friend, a family member, a spouse, or a stranger needed someone to uplift them and cheer them on. This companion always gave me just the right words to help the other person feel better. This companion always helped me help others be more and become more. The companion was my capacity to coach.

Leading up to my departure from the mortgage business, it seemed as if everything on the mortgage side was falling apart while everything on the coaching side was coming together. Coaching had been my companion for over thirty years. It came so naturally to me that I simply never connected the dots and considered making it my career.

For decades I fought against what came natural to me, because I had this notion that I had to build a "traditional" career. I fought against the current like a salmon going upstream. I know now that all the experiences I had along the way were leading to where I am today.

Now that I am doing what, in my heart, I know I should have been doing all along, I have inner peace. Helping people find happiness has always been my gift, my calling, my desire.

For over fifteen years I talked about writing a book to share my story and help others find their light at the end of the tunnel—not the light of an oncoming train, but real, uplifting, life-giving light. We are in charge of our lives. Stuff happens over which we have no control; but we, and we alone, control how we react. We can choose to be a victim, or we can choose to be victorious.

When we choose the victim route, we give up all of our control. Those who choose the victim route have to take and accept whatever they get.

Our society makes it easy to take this path. We have programs for this issue and that problem. We blame our circumstances and decisions on anything and everything outside of ourselves. We often don't even do anything for ourselves, as there are other people who will do it for us. Sadly, that has become socially acceptable.

The kind of flow generated by victim-supported society is nothing like the energetic life flow I am talking about. It's more like an uncomfortable flow on a life raft with no paddle, headed to a steep waterfall, hoping for the best. Who wants to ride in that boat?

What we want is the good flow where things simply fall into place. The kind of flow were the Universe delivers everything we need to move forward and live in harmony. The kind of flow where not just one thing feels good and right, but all aspects of life are in synch.

Since I made the decision to walk away from everything and follow my heart and passion, people take notice. Apparently, I exude happiness. How awesome is that?!

Going with the flow, your flow, does so much for your mind, body, soul, and spirit. Let your ego step out of the way and let the Universe guide you. Follow your path and your passion and watch doors open where you never imagined possible.

Listen to your inner voice, your gut instinct. The Universe puts little nuggets in your path and gives you just what you need in the moment. Those nuggets, or gifts, don't come in a nice box with a pretty bow. Most of the time, they are not obvious, and it takes some practice to recognize them. But they are there, all around you, waiting for you to enjoy.

For a lot of us it is hard to hear the whispers or to see the little nuggets because of all the background noise and chatter. We are pulled in a billion different directions and have so much on our mind: drop off the dog at the groomer, pick up the kids from school, stop at the grocery store, prepare for an important meeting. The list is endless.

It is important to disconnect. Quiet the noise and connect with your subconscious. Do you have a way to do that? Do you meditate, go for long walks, exercise, read, or pray? Find what works for you and do that. I like to meditate or go for a drive. When my body cooperates, I will go hiking. Do what you love!

Meditation puts me in flow. It gives me the calmness and the peace I need to step out of my ego and connect with my subconscious and the Universe. In calmness I stay centered and focused. My stress levels have shrunk, and situations that used to make me lose my cool are almost non-existent. I simply don't allow them to derail me.

Now I flow like the mighty Colorado River. I am forging my own glorious Grand Canyon within me. My happiness levels have shot through the roof. My energy vibrations attract more desirable circumstances and pleasant people to join me on the next steps of my journey.

Where does your flow take you? Are you going with your flow, or do you fight against it and get caught up in someone else's raging river? Do things come easily for you, or is your life a struggle and an uphill battle?

Take the time to quiet the noise so you can hear your subconscious whisper to you. Listen to your heart. What is it telling you?

Have you been playing the same tune in the background about something you wanted to do but didn't? Go with your flow. There will be no real struggle if you follow your dreams and follow your heart.

"I'm far more ready to go with the flow now because I am more accepting of myself."

Raquel Welch

Notes and Thoughts

What dreams, hopes, and desires are you flowing with?

Step 7: **Have Fun**

> *"Just play. Have fun. Enjoy the game."*
> Michael Jordan

fun
noun – fun /fuhn/
- what provides amusement or enjoyment

Michael Jordan sums it all up beautifully. It is so simple, yet so many have forgotten how to have fun and enjoy the game. Of course, we are not only talking about team sports here. We are talking about the game of life. Your life.

When was the last time you did something silly just because? When was the last time you did something just for you? When was the last time you just lay back and didn't worry about the dishes, laundry, or work? When was the last time you slept in without feeling guilty?

Life is about so much more than working and paying bills. All of that is necessary, but it is not the end all be all. It is merely one aspect of your life. Life has so much more to offer and for us to enjoy.

It's easy to get so focused on one thing that we forget about the rest. We can be consumed with things, situations, and people over whom we have zero control. We work ourselves up or get in arguments over politics, religion, and differing opinions. You know what they say about opinions: they are just like buttholes; everybody's got one.

Let people have their opinions, even if they don't coincide with yours. We are all different, with different views, beliefs, feelings, and emotions. It is okay to disagree! Compassion and understanding enhance our happiness.

Besides, getting worked up over different opinions is nonsense. It solves nothing. It disrupts our flow, throws us out of balance, and sucks the fun out of life. Getting worked up over events we see on the news does the same thing. I used to get so upset over things happening outside my sphere of influence. Some news would send me into depression. I took on the problems as if they were my own.

Now I send good vibes, energy, love, and light, and then I move on with my day. My heart goes out to those who suffer, but I no longer take on their suffering as my own. If I can do something to help and influence, I will. If it doesn't affect me directly and there is nothing I can do, I move on. It's not cold hearted; it's common sense.

If I put my energy into circumstances over which I have zero control or influence, it sucks energy away from the situations, organizations, and people for whom I CAN be of service. When we say *yes* to one thing, we say *no* to something else. When we say *yes* to the drama, the arguments, the worries, and things of that sort, we say *no* to having fun and enjoying life.

I am a bit of an empath. I take on the energy of others around me as if it were my own. If you ever feel sad or angry for no apparent reason, maybe you are an empath. In my days of depression, when I would pick up energy from people around me, it only added to my misery.

One of my best friends is a shaman. She taught me how to protect myself by building an energy shield around me. At first I chuckled, but once I learned that it works, WOW. I had been letting others zap the fun out of my experience and didn't even know it. (For more information, Mr. Google has some good links about energy shields).

For some, fun means partying, vacationing, doing extreme physical sports, sky diving, swimming with the sharks, dancing—the list is endless.

I have some physical limitations that prevent me from a lot of activities I used to enjoy. Being unable to walk for any significant distance, run, dance, or ride horseback sucked the fun out of life for me. For a long time, I was focused on all the things I could no longer do.

It pulled me down and kept me down. What was the point of attempting anything, knowing the physical pain would either prevent me from doing it in the first place or debilitate me for days afterwards? So, I took a seat on the sidelines, and life passed me by. I moped, wishing I could do what others could do, and felt sad and depressed because I couldn't.

I still can't, but now it's all right. Along my journey out of the abyss, I also learned to have fun and to enjoy the things I AM able to do. It simply required a mind shift. Instead of dwelling on what I cannot do, I focus on and enjoy those things I can do.

Shifting focus made all the difference for me. There are still times I wish I could do this thing or the other, and there probably always will be. It's all right. I have learned to focus on so many things I am still able to do and enjoy.

Life is amazing. The wonders and beauty of Mother Nature never cease to amaze me. I have found a love for people. Some folks say I love everybody when I tell them I love them. It is true. I do love all my fellow humans. There are a bunch I don't like or wouldn't hang out with, but I do love them.

Life is better and easier to deal with if you approach it with humor and fun. I think back to 2003, my "dark ages," when my husband was deployed, the kids were very young, and I was obese and in pain. I was overburdened with stress, and it was compounded by the whole Iraq thing. It was a very scary time for me.

And then I received the diagnosis of Multiple Sclerosis (MS). Let me tell you, denial IS a beautiful place! I never accepted the verdict, and I even started to poke fun at it. To me, MS stood for Mucho Special. Now I could laugh at it and move on with my life and not have this diagnosis take over. I was on medication for some years but never accepted the diagnosis. What I did do was cut stress out of my life as much as possible, I changed my eating habits, and I decided to have more fun. A few years ago, I stopped taking the meds all together. Over. Done. Moving on. Feeling fantastic. (I am not suggesting that you stop taking prescribed medication. That was a choice I made for myself, and I accept full responsibility and reward for it.)

Life has so much to offer—new experiences, adventures, people, business, learning. The list is endless. We simply have to stop every now and then and smell the roses. If literally smelling the roses makes you happy and feels fun, by all means, do it. For me, it means to stop, take a break from the grind, and have a little fun.

Go out for a nice dinner with your significant other or even by yourself. Go for a hike. Do the things that add to your happiness and recharge your batteries. Just like cell phone batteries, our inner energy source takes longer to recharge when we are completely depleted. Don't wait until your energy dies before you recharge.

Take care of yourself. Take a bubble bath, get a massage, a pedicure, a manicure, a facial, a haircut. Do physical activity you enjoy, go on vacation, do whatever it takes. Have fun while you are doing it and make plans for the next fun adventure.

Celebrate yourself. Enjoy being you. Be proud of yourself and all your accomplishments. It is easy to celebrate our big victories and overlook the small ones. But it is just as important to celebrate the small victories as it is to celebrate the big, in-your-face accomplishments.

Today, I celebrate making it through the store without falling. Today, I celebrate writing this last chapter in my book. Today, I celebrate getting up without hitting the snooze button on my alarm clock. Today, I celebrate keeping my cool when that person didn't let me merge onto the interstate. Today, I celebrate accomplishing my whole to-do list. Today, I celebrate being alive, above ground, vertical, and breathing. Today, I celebrate me.

Do you see how this works? My biggest accomplishment today is finishing the last chapter in this book I have wanted to write for almost twenty years. This is not an "invite the whole town" kind of celebration. (That will be my first book-signing event.) This is my private, quiet celebration, just for me. And to celebrate, I have treated myself to my favorite cup of coffee.

Inviting the whole town to celebrate your accomplishment is also valid. It is your celebration, and you deserve to celebrate in your own style. Whatever you do, have fun. Sometimes, we have to decide to have fun in spite of circumstances. There were countless times my husband and I had to attend military functions. They can be a lot of fun, or they can be utterly boring and suck the life right out of you. More times than not, I really didn't feel like going, but I didn't think I had a choice.

I always had two options. I could go and be miserable, bored out of my mind, and anti-social; or I could go, make it fun, mingle, and be entertained. Sometimes I had to focus on the food or the view, or just watch the people—no real effort, and I couldn't wait to leave. Other times I decided ahead of time to have fun. I didn't know what it would look like, I simply knew that I would have fun. And I did.

Choosing to have fun is a game changer. Sometimes we have fun because whatever we are doing is fun in itself. Other times, we have to consciously choose to have fun and make the best of it. Either way, everything is better when we are having fun.

Life flows when we are having fun. We are more relaxed and don't take things too seriously.

Having fun and being happy go hand in hand. Have you noticed, when you are happy you have more fun and when you have more fun you are happier? Funny how that works. (LOL— I am punny!)

Yes, happiness is a choice, and so is having fun. Life is short, so why not make the most of it and live it to the fullest? This is the only life you have in this body. Enjoy it. Go see the latest rage at the movie theatre and load up on the popcorn. Go on the dream vacation you have talked about for so long. Start the business you have wanted to start but were too worried to move forward. Ask that special someone out on a date. Heck, they just might say yes!

Stop worrying about the *what ifs* and *what's not*. Close your eyes and take that leap of faith. What do you have to lose? Yeah, it might not work out. Then again, it just might. Will it be uncomfortable? Possibly. Maybe not. Will there be setbacks? If so, learn from them. Try again. Move forward.

Trust yourself. Trust your instincts. Listen to your newly trained subconscious. Follow your heart. When it's time to decide what to do, try what works for me: Ask yourself if it will add to your happiness or take away from it. Knowing your answer makes your decision easy.

Let me clarify: I evaluate not only on the happiness and fun factor; I also evaluate whether this situation, opportunity, or person will add value to my life. Being happy and having fun is fantastic and is key to living a fulfilling life. You also need to give and receive value.

All the steps in this book are equally important, and you can follow them in any order that works for you. Hopefully, you find value in this little book and the seven easy steps to unleash your superpower. My intention is to add value wherever I go and whatever I do.

It is my honor to be a part of your tribe.

My wish for you:
- BE HAPPY
- HAVE FUN
- LIVE LIFE TO THE FULLEST

"It takes some balls to live life to the fullest."
Brock Lesnar

Notes and Thoughts

What fun things do you do to add to your happiness?

Notes and Thoughts

What fun things do you do to add to your happiness?

The 7 Steps to Happiness:

<u>Gratitude</u> – We always have something to be grateful for.

<u>Forgiveness</u> – In order to move forward, forgive yourself and others.

<u>Love Yourself</u> – You cannot pour from an empty cup.

<u>Nurture the Subconscious</u> – She is looking out for your best interest.

<u>Mindset</u> – It will either make you or break you.

<u>Go with the Flow</u> – Life is much easier if you do.

<u>Have Fun</u> – Might as well enjoy the ride.

These seven steps are each vitally important for a fulfilling life. Follow them in any order that works for you.

Above all, happiness is a choice. Choose you.
Choose HAPPY.

"Happiness: the most underused superpower we all possess."
Beenie Mann

About the Author

Beenie Mann is an Entrepreneur, Visionary, and Transformational Speaker. She is CEO of Matters of Perspective - an innovative coaching platform liberating people from the negative thinking patterns that keep them in a life that does not serve them.

Most of us live our lives through the lens of self-limiting beliefs. To ignite change most focus on changing the outside circumstances but Beenie teaches how to let happiness determine success, and how to break free of fear, shame and societal pressure.

Beenie's drive to elevate people has earned her the **Shield of Sparta** award from the National Infantry Association as well as the **Essayons Award** from the Army Engineer Association. She also won the **Outstanding Civilian Service Medal** from the Department of the Army. Her bestselling book **Happiness Matters** received 1st place at the 26th Annual CIPA-EVVY Awards.

Beenie has been assisting people in transforming their mindsets for more than 30 years. Her coaching platform is bridging the gap for the 95%.

To become part of the 5%, connect with Beenie today to get you moving forward https://MattersOfPerspective.com

Follow Beenie:

Facebook - https://www.facebook.com/mattersofperspective/
Twitter - https://twitter.com/beenie_mann
LinkedIn - https://www.linkedin.com/in/mattersofperspective/